A resource for parents, mentors, pastors, teachers and coaches.

PARENTING
Raising The Next Generation To Grow With Jesus

JEFF BAXTER

D1737732

PARENTING

DEDICATION

To all parents of every season striving to raise their kids to grow with Jesus.
This is a noble responsibility. May God bless and guide your every step.

CONTENTS

INTRO

Raising kids is challenging and maybe more difficult today than past decades. It is also extremely difficult to be a kid today. There are more distractions, temptations and challenges to growing up and becoming a responsible adult, especially as a faithful follower of Jesus.

This resource was birthed out of a workshop I have taught in a variety of churches over the years including my home church, Mission Hills (Missionhills.org). The goal is to equip you, parents (along with teaches, coaches, pastors and mentors), to have the tools and tactics necessary to be a faithful parent through the seasons. We are in a battle for the next generation and we must be intentional and focused on the journey.

My wife, Laurie and I have raised three wonderful kids (and are still parenting). This role never ends and times have changed, not because our kids have grown, but because child development and the surrounding culture have changed. At the time this resource was written we had two grown children in exciting stages of their lives and another in high school looking forward to the future. I am grateful they all are following Jesus, but it has had ups and downs along the way because of all the topics covered here.

I share this context to let you know we have stumbled along the path of parenting. We have not always seen things eye to eye as a couple, nor have we gotten it right with our kids, but we have worked it through and continue to do so. Did I mention all of my kids are still living at home. Yup, times have changed.

I pray this resource is helpful in giving you not only the big picture with what is happening with the next generation, but practical tips for you to use as you strive to help your children (and others in your community) grow into mature adults who are following Jesus closely. That's the goal and with God's help we can see it become a reality.

Grab a cup of coffee. Let's go on a journey together.

Jeff

PART ONE...

THE SITUATION BACK THEN MIGHT BE OUR SITUATION TODAY

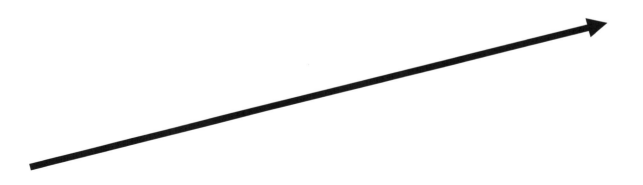

THE SITUATION BACK THEN MIGHT BE OUR SITUATION TODAY

13 People were bringing little children to Jesus for him to place his hands on them, but the disciples rebuked them. 14 When Jesus saw this, he was indignant. He said to them, "Let the little children come to me, and do not hinder them, for the kingdom of God belongs to such as these. 15 Truly I tell you, anyone who will not receive the kingdom of God like a little child will never enter it." 16 And he took the children in his arms, placed his hands on them and blessed them. - Mark 10:13-16

The situation back with Jesus, the disciples and families was not too different from our situation today in the culture we live in with some twists and turns. Parents had heard about this Jesus, a Rabbi and miracle worker. They brought their children to Jesus for a blessing. And those closest to Jesus, the disciples were preventing Jesus from connecting with kids. Can you imagine? You would think those closest to Jesus would get it, but apprarently they missed Jesus' purpose on the planet. Jesus was not happy with the disciples. He was indignant. That is not a good word expressing Jesus' feelings. Jesus would touch the children. Jesus' desire has always been to touch the next generation with love and care.

Question: Are we directly or indirectly preventing kids from coming to know Jesus and growing up because we don't understand them? What do you think?

PARENTING

PART TWO...

BACK TO BASICS

BACK TO BASICS

Biblical Foundation

Hear, O Israel: The Lord our God, the Lord is one. You shall love the LORD your God with all your heart and with all your soul and with all your might. And these words that I command you today shall be on your heart. You shall teach them diligently to your children, and shall talk of them when you sit in your house, and when you walk by the way, and when you lie down, and when you rise. You shall bind them as a sign on your hand, and they shall be as frontlets between your eyes. You shall write them on the doorposts of your house and on your gates. -Deuteronomy 6:4–9

NOTES: The beginning of these verses is called "The Shema" meaning "to hear" in Hebrew. It is a call for the Jewish people to raise their kids to love the One True God together, in community everywhere they went – sitting, walking, sleeping and getting up in the morning.

love.* See Deut. 4:37. all. That the Lord alone is Israel's God leads to the demand for Israel's exclusive and total devotion to him. heart … soul … might.** All Israelites in their total being are to love the Lord; "this is the great and first commandment" (Matt. 22:38). In Matt. 22:37, Mark 12:30, and Luke 10:27, Jesus also includes "mind." In early Hebrew, "heart" included what we call the "mind". "Might" indicates energy and ability.

on your heart. Cf. Deut 4:39. The demand is for a heart that totally loves the Lord. Deuteronomy anticipates the new covenant, when God's words will be truly and effectively written on the heart (Jer. 31:31–34; also Deut. 30:6–8).

The two pairs of opposites (**sit/walk, lie down/rise**) suggest any and every time, place, and activity. **bind them … write them.** Many Jews have fulfilled these commands literally with phylacteries (v. 8) and mezuzot (v. 9), i.e., boxes bound on the arm and forehead or attached to doorposts containing vv. 4–5 and other Scripture verses. See also Deut. 11:18–20.

PARENTING

PART THREE…

CHILDREN ARE A BLESSING

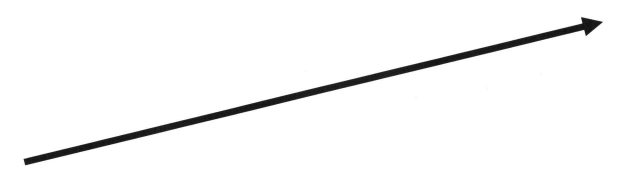

REMINDER…

CHILDREN ARE A BLESSING

Behold, children are a heritage from the LORD, the fruit of the womb a reward. Like arrows in the hand of a warrior are the children of one's youth. Blessed is the man who fills his quiver with them! He shall not be put to shame when he speaks with his enemies in the gate (Psalm 127:3–5).

Sometimes we need to be reminded that children are a blessing from God. Even when things are difficult, stressful and hurtful, kids are evidence of God's goodness.

Question: Write down some reasons why your kids are a blessing from the Lord.

NOTES: **children are a heritage from the LORD**, and therefore HIS gift to you, and yet husband and wife must do something in bringing the children into the world and in raising them to be faithful members of God's people. Here, the stress falls on **the children of one's youth**, now grown up and standing with their father **when he speaks with his enemies in the gate** (i.e., the place where justice was administered. It will be hard for the enemies (who are assumed to be unfaithful) to intimidate such a man.

PARENTING

PART FOUR…

TOUGH TO BE A PARENT TODAY. HARD TO BE A KID.

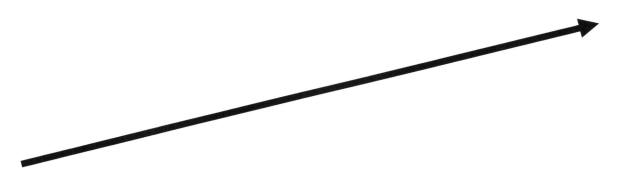

Tough to be a Parent Today
Harder to be a Kid Today

There is no doubt that parenting is very hard today. Times are different than they were in the 1970s, 1980s, 1990s and 2000s. But it is harder to be kid in a digitally saturated world.

Some respond by blaming kids, youth and young adults today.
Let's turn the tide.

Question: How do you think it is difficult to be a kid today, no matter their age?

CHURCH + FAMILY = PARTNERSHIP

BIG VISION FOR CHURCH AND FAMILY:

FOR EVERY KID
(Child, Middle Schooler, High Schooler and Young Adult)
to GROW WITH JESUS
THROUGH THE
SEASONS OF LIFE

Every single one of the next generation.
Grow **with**, not Grow **for**.
In every stage, phase and season of life…
For the longhaul.

It is a marathon of parenting, not a sprint.

PART FIVE…

HISTORY OF CHILDHOOD

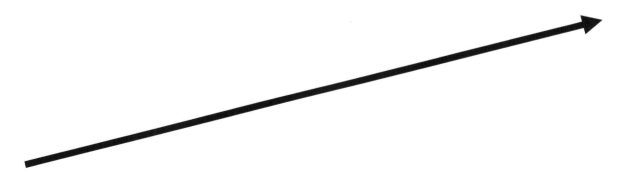

HISTORY OF CHILDHOOD

Once upon a time kids were Innocent, Safe, Free...
to sit in the back of the truck.

Today they are more Anxious, Cautious, Confined...
to the backseat buckled in for saftey.

Times have changed...

Question: Why do you think times have changed from decades ago? Write it down.

*Unknown Creator

*Developmental Questions By Year:

1yr   -Am I safe?
                         (Erikson - Trust/Mistrust)

2yr   -Am I able?
                         (Erikson - Autonomy/Shame-Doubt)

3-4yr   -Am I okay?
                         (Erikson - Initiative/Guilt)

Question: How have you intuitively seen your child wonder about these questions?

K-1st Grade   -Do I have your attention?

2nd-3rd   -Do I have what it takes?

4th-5th   -Do I have friends?

6th-8th   -Who do I like? Who likes me? Who am I?
                  (Erikson - Industry/Inferiority)

Question: How have you intuitively seen your child wonder about these questions?

9th   -Who Am I (continues)? Where do I belong?

10th   -Why should I believe in Jesus (or anything)?

11th   -Do My Choices Matter? What is my purpose?

12th   -What will I do when I grow up?
                                (Erikson - Intimacy/Isolation)

Young Adult   -Do I want adult responsibility?

Question: How have you intuitively seen your child wonder about these questions?

---

*Erik Erikson (1902–1994) was a German-American child psychoanalyst known for his theory on psychosocial development of human beings. He coined the phrase identity crisis. Erikson served as a professor at Harvard, University of California, Berkeley and Yale.

*https://www.simplypsychology.org/erik-erikson.html

MOTIVATIONS, RESPONSIBILITY AND HELP

Motivations:		Parent Responsibility:	Help Them:
0-4yrs -	**Safety**	Support their basic needs	Know God loves them Meet the Church
K-5th -	**Fun**	Help their interests	Trust God is faithful Get involved in the Church
6th-8th -	**Acceptance**	Affirm their identity in Jesus	Own their Faith Love the Church
9th-12th -	**Freedom**	Equip for the future	Grow to own faith Discover purpose

Connection to the Church is Vital!

Question: How are you connecting your child to church? How is your family worshipping and serving in the church community?

PARENTING

PART SIX…

HISTORY OF ADOLESCENCE

HISTORY OF ADOLESCENCE
11-26ish years…
Yup! Times have changed! It is longer!

Adolescere (Latin) - "To Grow Up"

GOAL of Adolescence:

Individuation - Process of becoming a unique individual.

TASKS OF INDIVIDUATION (Adolescence)

Every child ages 11-25ish are intuitively asking these three questions over and over…

1. **Identity** - Who Am I?

2. **Autonomy** - Do I matter?

3. **Belonging** - Does anyone care about me for me?

Question: Where have you experienced your child struggling with these three questions? (Who Am I?, Do I matter?, Does anyone care about me for me?)

TIMING AND DURATION

Ages of Adolescence*

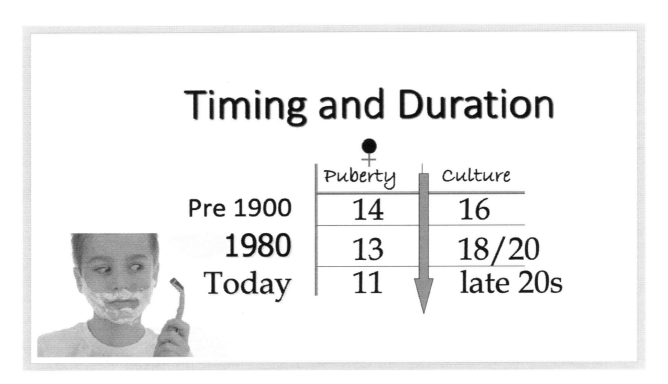

*Adolescence "begins with biology and ends in culture." In other words, it is easy to determine the start, but harder to see the transition into becoming a full responsible adult.

Adolescent Journey Today

> "If you think of the teenage brain as a car, today's adolescents acquire an accelerator a long time before they can steer and brake."
> - Wall Street Journal, Alison Gopnik, Professor/Psychologist

Question: Have you experienced adolescence getting longer in today's kids? Where? How?

*BOOK: *The Hurried Child*, David Elkind PhD (Revisions 1981,2001,2006)

PART SEVEN…

COMMUNITY LACKING

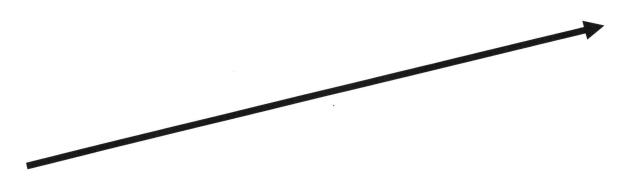

COMMUNITY LACKING

The Loss of Community

1. Adults used to believe that **ALL** kids were **THEIR** kids.

2. Adults used to see their **PRIMARY** role as facilitating children becoming adults.

3. Adults once saw kids as **ASSETS**, not **LIABILITIES** because they are worth the effort.

4. Adults used to **"BE THERE"** for kids more than just driving kids there.

Question: Have you seen the breakdown of community not surrounding the next generation? Where? How?

How Can The Community Help?

1-Build scaffolding of relationships.

2-Adding more Christ-following adults in kids lives.

3-Healthy brain development is healthy attachment.

Question: Who are the relationships in your kid's life besides you? Do you have 5 other Jesus Following adults who are in their life? Where could you find them?

*Resource: *40 Developmental Assets*, Search Insitute.

Result: Systemic Abandonment in Adolescence

Systemic = in a systematic way…
Abandonment = cease to support…

AS A RESULT…

1   **Adolescents lie in an underground world.**

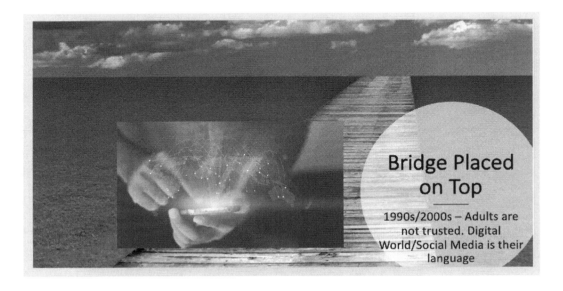

Bridge Placed
on Top

1990s/2000s – Adults are
not trusted. Digital
World/Social Media is their
language

AS A RESULT...

2 Adolescents live out multiple selves (identities).

"Adolescents develop a proliferation of selves that vary as a function of the social context. These include self with father, mother, close friend, romantic partner, peers, as well as the self in the role of student, on the job, and as athlete...a critical developmental task of adolescence, therefore, is the construction of multiple selves in different roles and relationships." -Susan Harter, "Complexity of Self in Adolescence"

Question: Have you experienced your child or other kids "trying on different selves" to figure out who they are? What have they done?

AS A RESULT...

3   "Successful" kids learn to adapt.

"'Successful' students learn to devise various strategies to stay ahead of their peers and to **please** those in power positions [teachers, coaches, administration, pastors]; unsuccessful students, for a variety of reasons, were not as adept at **playing** the survival game." -Denise Clark Pope, PhD, *Doing School*

"Why are children of privilege, in record numbers, having an extraordinary difficult time completing the most fundamental task of adolescence - the development of autonomy and a healthy sense of self?" -Madeline Levine, PhD, *The Price of Privilege*

AS A RESULT...

4 Peers and Friendships have changed*

Cliques: groups of students who established their place on the teen pecking order (popular group, the jocks, the nerds, valley girls). Larger categories of students.

Clusters: Smaller groupings of friends which navigate as a unit in the complex network of social interdependence with high loyalty like a family. They keep one another safe.

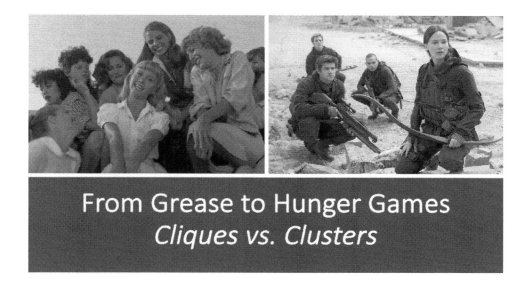

From Grease to Hunger Games
Cliques vs. Clusters

*BOOK: Chap Clark, *Hurt: Inside the World of Today's Teenagers.*

AS A RESULT...

5 More Freedoms, Dangers, Stressers.

*Unknown Creator

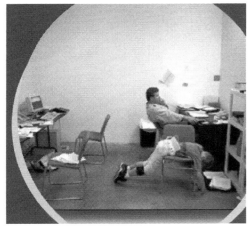

*Unknown Creator

PARENTING

PART EIGHT…

WHAT ARE WE TO DO? WHAT IS OUR ROLE AS PARENTS?

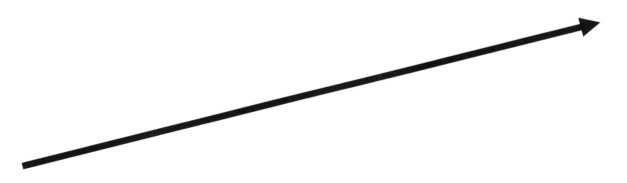

WHAT ARE WE TO DO?
WHAT IS OUR ROLE AS PARENTS?

Question: Who are you identifying with these days?

Ferris
Cameron
Rooney

Why?

*If you have not seen *Ferris Bueller's Day Off,* put everything down and watch it!

*Unknown Creator, From Movie *Ferris Bueller's Day Off*

PARENTING THROUGH THE SEASONS

ROLES

SHERPA - Carrying the weight and plotting the path for your child.
RABBI - Teaching your child Biblical Principles today for the future.
SAGE - Ready to impart wisdom as a veteran.

*Unknown Creators

The key is to descern when to dance between the roles...

Question: What season and role in parenting are you in today? What is easy and what is hard about this role?

FUTURE GOAL IN PARENTING: Proverbs 22:6

Train up a child in the way he should go; even when he is old he will not depart from it.

NOTES: Train up a child. This proverb, founded on the covenant with Abraham (cf. Gen. 18:19), encourages parents to "train" (i.e., to "dedicate" or "initiate"; this is the sense of the word in Deut. 20:5; cf. Ezra 6:16) their children in the way (i.e., the right moral orientation) by pointing to the kinds of conduct that please or displease the Lord, and to the normal outcome of each kind of conduct. The training will include love and instruction as well as "the rod of discipline" (Prov. 22:15).

PARENTS ARE TEACHERS: Ephesians 6:1–4

Children, obey your parents in the Lord, for this is right. "Honor your father and mother" (this is the first commandment with a promise), "that it may go well with you and that you may live long in the land." Fathers, do not provoke your children to anger, but bring them up in the discipline and instruction of the Lord.

> **NOTES: Fathers (and Mothers).** As earlier, Paul begins his admonition with a negative action to avoid, followed by a positive action to develop. Paul addresses the responsibility of fathers in particular, though this does not diminish the contribution of mothers in these areas (see Proverbs 31). **provoke ... to anger.** Obedient children are particularly vulnerable, so a domineering and thoughtless father's actions would be discouraging to them (Col. 3:21). **bring them up**. Parents play a crucial, God-ordained role in the discipleship of their children "in the Lord" (Eph. 6:1); see Deut. 6:1–9. Parental discipleship **in the discipline and instruction of the Lord** should center on the kinds of practices already outlined in Ephesians 4–5.

DIRECTING OUR KIDS: Hebrews 12:7–11

It is for discipline that you have to endure. God is treating you as sons. For what son is there whom his father does not discipline? If you are left without discipline, in which all have participated, then you are illegitimate children and not sons. Besides this, we have had earthly fathers who disciplined us and we respected them. Shall we not much more be subject to the Father of spirits and live? For they disciplined us for a short time as it seemed best to them, but he disciplines us for our good, that we may share his holiness. For the moment all discipline seems painful rather than pleasant, but later it yields the peaceful fruit of righteousness to those who have been trained by it.

> **NOTES: exhortation that addresses you as sons.** God is viewed as speaking through the proverb; God's discipline proves that he considers believers to be his sons (on sonship, see Heb. 2:10), since God **chastises every son whom he receives** (Heb. 12:6; see Heb. 12:7–8). **Discipline** (Gk. *paideia*) was a common term for childrearing through instruction, training, and correction; however, here Hebrews focuses on the call for perseverance (**endure** in Heb. 12:7) in the painful tests of life (Heb. 12: 11). These tests are to their benefit, prove their sonship, and require a response of perseverance. The readers, then, should not be discouraged.
>
> This lesser-to-greater analogy from the readers' own childhood training shows that it is appropriate for the heavenly Father to discipline, and it calls for a response of respect and submission; as a loving Father, the Lord always disciplines his children **for** their **good**.

GOD IS OUR EXAMPLE: Psalm 103:13

As a father shows compassion to his children, so the LORD shows compassion to those who fear him.

NOTES: God is a **father** to his people as a whole (Ex. 4:22–23), and to the particular faithful members (Prov. 3:12). Of course many human fathers fail to embody this idea; this image assumes that biblically informed people have an intuition of what fathers ideally should be like. But it also serves as a goal for faithful fathers: they will seek more and more to be the kind of father who shows **compassion to his children.**

PARENTS ENCOURAGE: Colossians 3:20–21

Children, obey your parents in everything, for this pleases the Lord. Fathers, do not provoke your children, lest they become discouraged.

NOTES: Paul's words to children reflect the fifth commandment (Ex. 20:12). **do not provoke your children**. Men are urged to restrain their anger and any other attitudes that can embitter their children (cf. Eph. 6:4), lest they despair of pleasing their parents.

PARENTING

PART NINE...

WHAT IS THE ROLE OF PARENTS THROUGH THE SEASONS?

WHAT IS THE ROLE OF PARENTS THROUGH THE SEASONS?

1. Offering Understanding. Their perception is reality, so it is always better to understand the situation they are in.

2. Offer Compassion. Be present and show support.

3. Provide Boundaries. Every developmental stage needs guardrails for following Jesus.

4. Chart the Course & Guide The Course. Provide a map and be there for them along the way.

Question: How are you practically doing each of the above? Where has it worked? What can you do to improve?

PARENTING

PART TEN...

KIDS, YOUTH AND YOUNG ADULTS ARE STRESSED OUT!

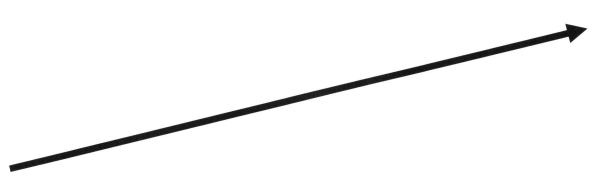

KIDS, YOUTH AND YOUNG ADULTS ARE STRESSED OUT!

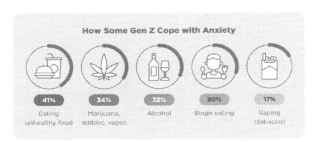

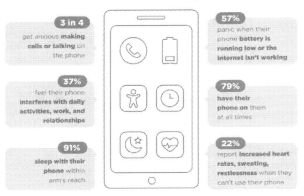

70% of millennials would say they are experiencing some level of burnout.

54% are chronically lonely.

30% of millennials and Gen Z state they experience disruptive anxiety and depression.

-Ryan Pendell, "Millennials Are Burning Out"

"People who are stressed are, in a word, egocentric, though not necessarily conceited or prideful. They have little opportunity to consider the needs and interest of others." - David Elkind, *The Hurried Child*

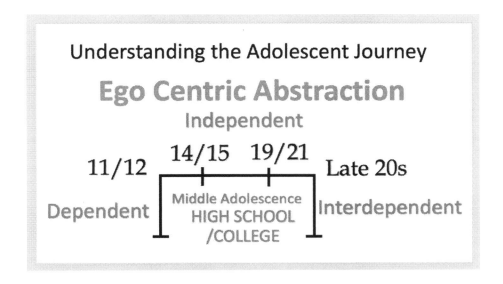

PART ELEVEN...

WHY THIS ALL MATTERS TO US AND THE CHURCH?

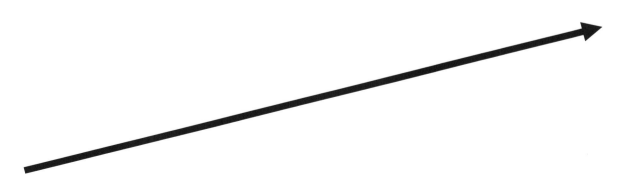

WHY THIS ALL MATTERS TO US AND THE CHURCH?

Adolescents are walking a tightrope and need to be surrounded by caring adults, especially Jesus following adults. This journey begins as they enter adolescence around 11 years old and completes in their 20's when they are a responsible adult. The local church plays a vital role in this process.

What a child and adolescent *needs...*

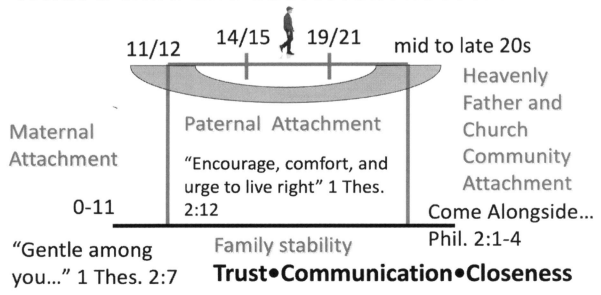

PARENTING

PARENT ROLE:

OVERVIEW OF WHAT IS COMING…

Parent Role: Sherpa
0-4 years - DELIGHT

Parent Role: Sherpa to Rabbi
K-5th Grade - DISCOVER
6th-8th - DECIDE

Parent Role: Rabbi to Sage
9th-12th - DRIVE
Post High School - DEVELOP

PARENTING

PART TWELVE…

HOW DO WE FUEL FAITH IN THE NEXT GEN?

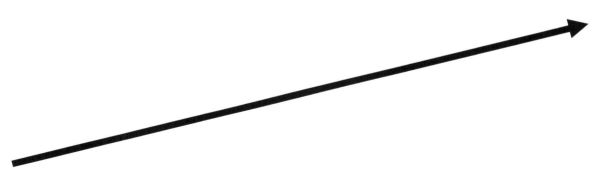

HOW DO WE FUEL FAITH IN THE NEXT GEN?

Parent Role: SHERPA

0-4 years - DELIGHT (*Maternal Attachment)

Know how much Jesus loves them and connect with the church community

Pray with them
Encourage them to pray
Read the Bible to them
Encourage them with God's love
Sing Worship Songs with them
Connect to a Bible believing/teaching and Next Gen focused church

*Naturally, children are connected to their mother's in the early stages of life development starting in the womb (Maternal Attachment)

LOTS OF PLAY (Birth-4yrs)

Children who use their imagination and 'play pretend' in safe environments are able to learn about their emotions, what interests them, and how to adapt to situations. When children play with each other, they are given the opportunity to learn how to interact with others and behave in various social situations.

Be sure to give your child plenty of time and space to play. There are 6 stages of play during early childhood, all of which are important for your child's development. All of the stages of play involve exploring, being creative, and having fun. This list explains how children's play changes by age as they grow and develop social skills.

Unoccupied Play (Birth-3 Months)
At this stage baby is just making a lot of movements with their arms, legs, hands, feet, etc. They are learning about and discovering how their body moves.

Solitary Play (Birth-2 Years)
This is the stage when a child plays alone. They are not interested in playing with others quite yet.

Spectator/Onlooker Behavior (2 Years)
During this stage a child begins to watch other children playing but does not play with them.

Parallel Play (2+ Years)
When a child plays alongside or near others but does not play with them this stage is referred to as parallel play.

Associate Play (3-4 Years)
When a child starts to interact with others during play, but there is not a large amount of interaction at this stage. A child might be doing an activity related to the kids around him, but might not actually be interacting with another child. For example, kids might all be playing on the same piece of playground equipment but all doing different things like climbing, swinging, etc.

Cooperative Play (4+ Years)
When a child plays together with others and has interest in both the activity and other children involved in playing they are participating in cooperative play.

HOW OLD ARE YOUR KIDS?

HOW CAN YOU PLAY WITH THEM?

Parent Role: SHERPA to RABBI

K-5th Grade - DISCOVER
Trust Jesus and experience the church community

Pray with them
Encourage them to Pray
Help them to Trust God
Pick out a Bible with them that is theirs
Read the Bible together
Ask questions about Bible stories
Memorize Bible verses together
Share your personal faith story
Serve as a family in the church community

6th-8th - DECIDE (*Paternal Attachment)

Grab faith in Jesus and value the church community

Encourage them to serve in the church community
Allow them to ask difficult questions about life, God and the Bible
Help them develop a personal time alone with Jesus each day
Help them prioritize student ministry / small group in their church community
Help them pick trustworthy friends at this stage
Attend the worship service at church together
If they haven't already, ask them if they are ready to trust Jesus as their Savior

COMMUNICATION WITH GRACE IS KEY!

*Dad's role in the life of his child during adolescence (Paternal Attachment) is very important to development. This is not the time to check out and back away, but to lean in with Truth and Grace equaling love.

Parent Role: RABBI to SAGE

9th-12th - **DRIVE**

Keep growing in faith and discover purpose with church community

Continue to serve in the church community where they are excited
Encourage them to regularly pray to God and read their Bible
Help them wrestle with their faith with doubts and fears
Welcome questions about God
Give them Biblical principles to live by
Show authentic grace and truth equaling love
Encourage them to participate in an Outreach trip
Dream about the future with them
Help them make bigger commitments

KEEP COMMUNICATION LINES OPEN!

Parent Role: SAGE

Post High School - **DEVELOP**

Connect purpose to life decisions like Training/College, Dating/Marriage, Jobs/Career

Support and be available as a friend
Coach when invited in
Keep encouraging their relationship with Jesus

*Erik Erikson Development Stages:

The stages that make up his theory are as follows:

- Stage 1: <u>Trust vs. Mistrust</u> (Infancy from birth to 18 months)
- Stage 2: <u>Autonomy vs. Shame and Doubt</u> (Toddler years from 18 months to three years)
- Stage 3: <u>Initiative vs. Guilt</u> (Preschool years from three to five)
- Stage 4: <u>Industry vs. Inferiority</u> (Middle school years from six to 11)
- Stage 5: <u>Identity vs. Confusion</u> (Teen years from 12 to 18)
- Stage 6: <u>Intimacy vs. Isolation</u> (Young adult years from 18 to 40)
- Stage 7: <u>Generativity vs. Stagnation</u> (Middle age from 40 to 65)
- Stage 8: <u>Integrity vs. Despair</u> (Older adulthood from 65 to death)

DETAILS:

Infancy - Basic Trust vs. Basic Mistrust - Hope: The primary relationship (or social institution) of this <u>first stage is the mother.</u> The infant needs to be fed (and traditionally this was only breast-feeding), comforted, and protected. As we have seen in earlier chapters, the child does not necessarily recognize that the mother is a separate person, so the bond between them is extraordinarily intimate. It is inevitable, however, that the child will experience discomfort and pain, and that the mother will not be able to immediately attend to every need. In such times of distress, the child who mostly trusts in the care of their mother will be able to hope that the care is coming.

As a young child develops a sense of autonomy, they begin to do more for themselves.

*Reference: *Very Well Mind*

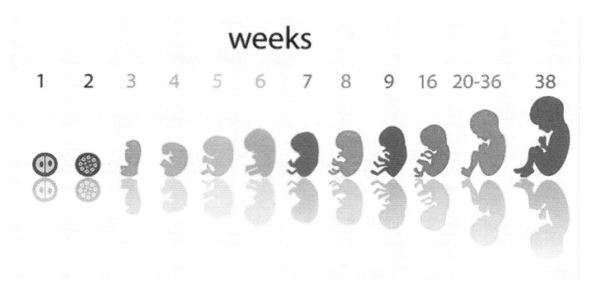

Early Childhood - Autonomy vs. Shame, Doubt - Will: At this stage, <u>both parents</u> become the primary social institution. As young children develop the ability to walk and talk they begin to do many things for themselves. However, their actions often lead to restrictions, as they experience the categorical rules of "yes and no," "right and wrong," or "good and bad." Shame is the consequence of being told that one is bad or wrong. Doubt arises when the child is unsure. As they develop their will power, i.e., their exercise of free will, they may not be sure what to do in a certain situation. A child who has been supported in exercising their autonomy will develop the will power to restrain themselves without experiencing shame or doubt. For example, they will learn not to run out into the busy street, and even feel good about their ability to take care of and protect themselves. It is often fascinating to watch a young child demonstrate this protectiveness when they interact with an even younger child. One can easily see the satisfaction in understanding rules and guidelines as, say, an eight-year old looks after a two-year old cousin.

Play Age - Initiative vs. Guilt - Purpose: The <u>entire family</u> (e.g., siblings, grandparents, etc.) provides the social context for this developmental stage. As the child of age three or four years old becomes able to do much more, and to do so more vigorously, they begin to realize something of what is expected of them as adults. So, they being to play with other children, older children, and to play games that mimic things done by adults. This helps them to develop a sense of purpose, and to pursue valued goals and skills. Excessive initiative, especially when combined with autonomy, can lead to problems such as rivalry and jealousy, especially with younger siblings. It can also lead to aggressive manipulation or coercion. Consequently, the child can begin to feel guilty about their actions, especially if they are punished.

As children grow a little older, they begin to mimic what they see being done by older children and adults.

School Age - Industry vs. Inferiority - Competence: The social institutions relevant to this stage now move outside the family, including the neighborhood, community, and schools. It is one thing to play adult roles, such as in the previous stage, but in this stage the child actually begins the process of preparing to be a caretaker and provider for others, such as their own children. In all cultures, according to Erikson, at this age (beginning at 5 to 6 years old) children receive some form of systematic training, and they also learn eagerly from older children. Unfortunately, some children are not as successful as others, particularly in the restrictive learning environment of schools. Keep in mind that Erikson was trained in the Montessori style of education, which emphasizes free exploration and active learning, at each child's own pace (Lillard & Jessen, 2003; Spietz, 1991). If children are indeed successful, if they are given the freedom to learn, they will develop a sense of competence, which will help them to persevere when faced with more challenging tasks.

Adolescence - Identity vs. Role Diffusion, Confusion - Fidelity: The family finally loses its place of primacy as a social institution, as peer groups become the most significant social institutions. According to Erikson, childhood comes to an end when a person has developed the skills and tools to proceed into adulthood. First, however, there is the period in which one's body changes from a child to an adult: **puberty**. Known psychologically as adolescence, it is a period in which each person must determine how they will fit their particular skills into the adult world of their culture. This requires forming one's identity. The fidelity that Erikson speaks of refers to the ability to remain true to oneself, and to one's significant others. This period is easiest for children who are gifted and well trained in the pursuit of clear goals, and also for children who receive a good deal of affirmation from their peers.

The pursuit of one's identity can be quite challenging, and we will examine identity in more detail in the next section. But first, one way to cope with the challenge of forming one's identity is to stop doing it for a while, something Erikson called a psychosocial **moratorium** (Erikson, 1959) (today called a "gap year"). A moratorium is a break that one takes in life before committing oneself to a career. Some people serve in the military or the Peace Corps before coming home and taking their place in the community. Some travel, and try to "see the world," before starting college. Erikson considered the moratorium to be a natural and, in many cases, quite productive activity.

Young Adulthood - Intimacy vs. Isolation - Love: With the onset of adulthood, the most significant social factors become partners in friendship, competition, and cooperation. Once an individual has consolidated their own identity, they are capable of the self-abandonment necessary for intimate affiliations, or inspiring encounters. Love is the mutual devotion of two people. Individuals who are unsuccessful in making intimate contacts are at risk for exaggerating their isolation, which brings with it the danger of not making any new contacts that might lead to the very intimate relationship they are lacking.

Question: What did you learn about Erikson's Developmental Stages? What was helpful? What can you apply to your relationship with your kids?

PART THIRTEEN...

TACKLING TECHNOLOGY

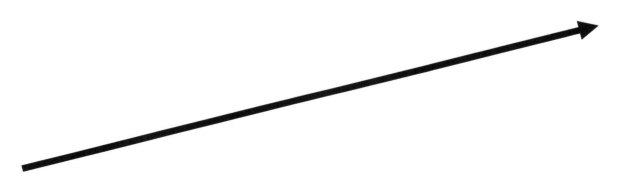

TACKLING TECHNOLOGY

THE GENERATIONS AND TECHNOLOGY *(with ages as of 2024)*

The Silent Generation (born 1928-1945) *(ages 79-96)*
Radio, Television, Typewriters, Rotary Telephones, and early Calculators.

Baby Boomers (born 1946-1964) *(ages 60-78)*
First **personal computers** and the concept of the **internet** was born.

Generation X - Busters (born 1965-1980) *(ages 44-59)*
Consumer electronics - video game consoles, VCRs, and **cordless phones.** As they entered adulthood, **the first mobile phones**, **the emergence of the World Wide Web**.

Generation Y - Millennials (born 1981-1996) *(ages 28-43)*
The internet and mobile technologies were rapidly developing. They witnessed the transformation **from dial-up internet to high-speed broadband** and were early adopters of **social media platforms** like Facebook and Twitter. Started embracing services like **Uber and Airbnb.**

Generation Z – Digital Natives (born 1997-2012) *(ages 12-27)*
Technology was seamlessly integrated into their lives. They never experienced a world without **smartphones, tablets, and social media. TikTok** has taken off with this generation.

Generation Alpha (born 2013-2025) *(ages 0-11)* - As the youngest generation, Generation Alpha is **currently shaping its relationship with technology**. They are growing up surrounded by smart devices, AI assistants, and augmented reality experiences. This generation is **expected to be even more tech-savvy and digitally fluent than its predecessors.**

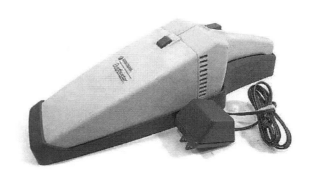

*Unknown creators

Parent Role: Sherpa

0-4 years - DELIGHT

Give them positive experiences

Use tools when needed, but not dependent on them
Partner with other Parents for Best Practices
Be present, don't just take pictures/video
Limit the screen time per day
Consider a protection plan
Create screen free zones (like meals and bedrooms)
Play video games together

*Unknown creator

Parent Role: Sherpa to Rabbi

K-5th Grade - DISCOVER

Grow in values and skills

Talk about technology
Establish worldwide web boundaries (no need to talk to google, Siri or Youtube without parents)
Use technology to share nostalgia (music videos)
Make technology social (groups for family)
Establish rules for online sharing (social media, posts, texting)
Ask questions to stay current (have you seen anything that surprised you?)
Let me show you how it works

*Unknown Creator or location

6th-8th - **DECIDE**

Create limits and social boundaries

Think about when to buy a Smart Phone
Make clear boundaries and limits
Share accounts (iTunes)
Use technology for your relationship (texting, social media)
Research current social media
Start social media accounts together
Tell child you can monitor all social media and texting
Be sensitive to how often you should engage their posts

The primary way communication happens with friends is through social media (i.e. Snapchat)

Parent Role: Rabbi to Sage

9th-12th - DRIVE

Control technology. Don't let it control you.

Ask what apps and platforms they are using weekly
Use technology to glorify God
Use technology to learn about hobbies (YouTube, TikTok)
Consider sharing the bill (music, cell phone, gaming)
Create clear expectations about using technology while driving (texting, music)
Research online education options
Never let a high schooler get an online dating App
Share online family calendar
Discuss boundaries and limitations
Talk about college online applications
Talk about the future with technology

KEEP COMMUNICATION LINES OPEN!

Post High School - DEVELOP

Keep leveraging the positive and drop the negative

Continue to coach for good habits
Be available for conversations

PARENTING

PART FOURTEEN…

HOW DO WE HELP THE NEXT GEN WITH SEXUAL INTEGRITY?

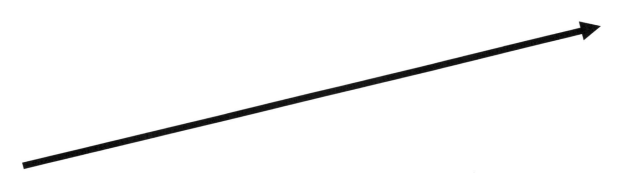

HOW DO WE HELP THE NEXT GEN WITH SEXUAL INTEGRITY

Parent Role: Sherpa

0-4 years - DELIGHT

General introduction to the body God gave them

Share with them God loves them
Begin to introduce body part names
Share the difference between boys and girls
Set up privacy boundaries / coach privacy
Answer general questions with general answers
Encourage healthy growth

Parent Role: Sherpa to Rabbi

K-5th Grade - DISCOVER

Let them know how their body works

Talk about physical boundaries
Help with relational skills like love, kindness and respect
Have conversation about body changes
Have conversations about healthy friendships
Talk about sexual activity and pornography
Talk about vocabulary and what they are hearing
Talk about beauty and modesty

6th-8th - **DECIDE**

Help them grow in respecting themselves

Talk about the changes occurring physically
Talk about attraction to the opposite sex
Set up dating expectations to honor God with your body
Take their feelings seriously
Stay connected to their world
Keep an eye on their social media accounts
Negotiate boundaries around physicality

KEEP COMMUNICATION LINES OPEN!

Parent Role: Rabbi to Sage

9th-12th - DRIVE

Negotiate healthy relationships

Discuss dating values and expectations
Discuss how to treat and talk about the other sex
Talk about God's boundaries and marriage expectations
Surround kids with other likeminded adult mentors
Stay calm and loving no matter what they share with you
Ask questions and have conversations around body image
Stay aware of what your child is feeling
Stay connected on social media

*Unknown Creator

Post High School - **DEVELOP**

Coach for the future

Continue to encourage living fully for God with their bodies
Stay connected on social media
Be available for conversations when they bring them up

PARENTING

PART FIFTEEN...

ADOPTIVE COMMUNITY

*ADOPTIVE COMMUNITY

The church community should be the place where the next generation is loved, cared for with Truth and Grace equalling love. It is an adoptive community where everyone converges on the next generation with congruence in message.

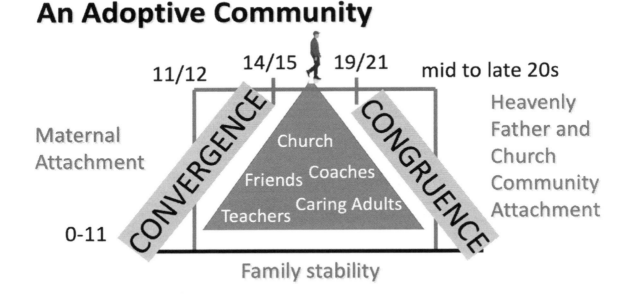

BOOK: *Adoptive Church* - Chap Clark

Mark the Moments (Family / Church):

- Baby Dedication (Months)
- First Day of School (4/5 yrs)
- Trusted Jesus as Savior / Baptism
- Become Adolescent (Puberty) (11/12 yrs Girls, 13/14 yrs Boys)
- Driver's License (HS) (16 yrs)
- Graduation (HS) (18 yrs)
- Graduation / Career Decisions (18+ yrs)

Question: How is your family marking the moments involving the church community in celebration and accountability as you raise your child to love Jesus?

MORE TIPS

1. **Be the Adult** – You are the fully individuated one. Act like it even in the high stress conversations.

2. **Think Long Haul** – This is a marathon, not a sprint.

3. **Be a 'student' of your child** – Keep learning about them.

4. **Say 'I am sorry' lots** – This models humility and grace.

5. **Be flexible, yet organized** – Always think ahead, but realize things can change in a moment with your child.

6. **Transition from Sherpa to Rabbi to Sage** – Know your role in each season.

GOAL OF PARENTING

To **love** in such a way that your child is **convinced** that he/she is fully **capable** of making a positive **impact** in the world for **Jesus**.

Question: Write down your goal for parenting? What is your plan to accomplish the overall BIG GOAL?

PART SIXTEEN...

MORE BIG TIPS

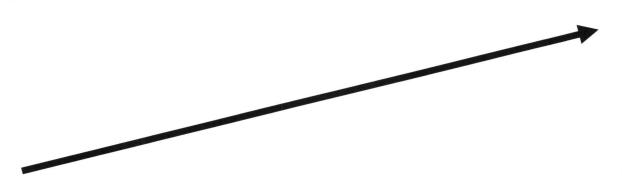

MORE BIG TIPS
From Jeff Baxter's Book

Overall Parenting Practices Through All The Seasons:

- Pass Passion
- Grow in Grace
- Hold onto Holiness
- Tell The Truth
- Be Amazed By God

Question: How are you currently showing and telling these to your child?

BOOK: Jeff Baxter, *Go & Grow (Parent & Mentor Edition and Student Edition): Five Keys To Moving Your Faith Forward And Adulting In The Real World*

BOOK OUTLINE WITH CHAPTERS:

KEY ONE: PASS PASSION

Belief: Trust in Jesus, Prayer: Talking with God, Doubt: Those Uncertain Moments

KEY TWO: GROW IN GRACE

Grace: The Priceless Gift, Stress: Managing the Pressure, Mentoring: Spiritual Growth with Others

KEY THREE: HOLD ONTO HOLINESS

Responsibility: Getting Wisdom, Morality: Smart Behavior, Friends: Finding and Keeping Them, Dating and Sex: Searching For A Spouse

KEY FOUR: TELL THE TRUTH

Worldview: Owning Your Faith, Bible: Your Authority, Bible: The Whole Story

KEY FIVE: BE AMAZED BY GOD

God's Creation: The Start of Awe, God's Will: His Design For You, Your Local Church: Finding and Investing in a Local Family

PART SEVENTEEN…

THE END IN MIND

THE END IN MIND

Grandparenting! Proverbs 17:6

Grandchildren are the crown of the aged, and the glory of children is their fathers.

LEGACY LEAVING

Psalm 71:15-18

15 My mouth will tell of your righteous deeds, of your saving acts all day long—though I know not how to relate them all. 16 I will come and proclaim your mighty acts, Sovereign Lord; I will proclaim your righteous deeds, yours alone. 17 Since my youth, God, you have taught me, and to this day I declare your marvelous deeds. 18 Even when I am old and gray, do not forsake me, my God, till I declare your power to the next generation, your mighty acts to all who are to come.

REVIEW

Parent Role: Sherpa

0-4 years **- DELIGHT**

Parent Role: Sherpa to Rabbi

K-5th Grade - **DISCOVER**

6th-8th - **DECIDE**

Parent Role: Rabbi to Sage

9th-12th - **DRIVE**

Post High School - **DEVELOP**

Five Themes To Frame Next Gen Discipleship
**Barna Research Study*

1. The Church Must Help Younger Generations Wisely Navigate Screen Time

2. The Church Must Integrate Its Response to Injustice into Student Ministry

3. The Church Must Address Issues of Loneliness and Anxiety in Young Adults

4. The Church Must Support and Encourage Resilient Disciples to Grow Their Faith

5. The Church Must Reframe the Notion of Outreach and Faith-Sharing with the Next Gen

RESOURCE: BARNA, *Five Themes To Frame Next Gen Discipleship (barna.com)*

PARENTING

PARENTING

NOTE PAGES

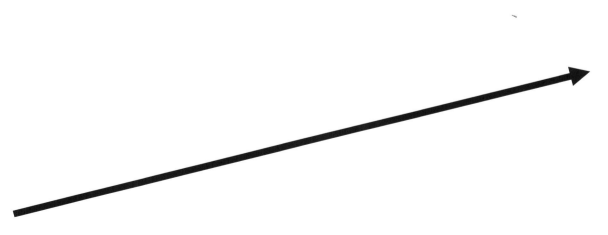

NOTES

NOTES

NOTES

NOTES

NOTES

NOTES

NOTES

NOTES

NOTES

NOTES

PARENTING

RESOURCES / REFERENCES

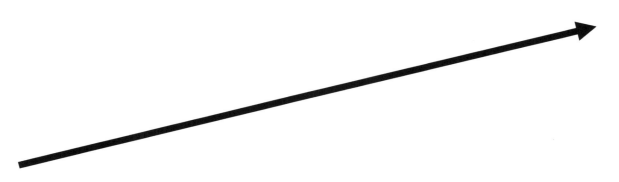

RESOURCES / REFERENCES:

Parenting
Growing With - Kara Powell, Steven Argue
Shepherding a Child's Heart - Tedd Tripp
Parenting Beyond Your Capacity - Reggie Joiner, Carey Nieuwhof
Boundaries with Teens - John Townsend
It's Personal - Virginia Ward, Reggie Joiner, Kristen Ivy
Caught In Between: Engage Your Preteens Before They Check Out - Dan Scott

Next Gen Culture
The Slow Fade - Reggie Joiner, Chuck Bomar, Abbie Smith
You Lost Me - David Kinnaman (Barna Research)
UnChristian - David Kinnaman with Gabe Lyons (Barna Research)
The Next Christians - Gabe Lyons
Faith For Exiles - David Kinnaman and Mark Matlock

Adolescent Development and Generations
Hurt: Inside the World of Today's Teenagers - Chap Clark
When Kids Hurt: Helping Adults Navigate the Adolescent Maze - Chap Clark, Steve Rabey
Generation Z Unfiltered - Tim Elmore, Andrew McPeak
Meet Generation Z - James Emery White

Church
Growing Young - Kara Powell, Jake Mulder, Brad Griffin
Adoptive Church - Chap Clark

Jeff Baxter Books for Parents (Strategy and Discipleship)
Go & Grow (Parent & Mentor Edition and Student Edition): Five Keys To Moving Your Faith Forward And Adulting In The Real World
Creating Healthy Churches: What Repairing Streams Has Taught Me About Healing The Church
Exploring Israel: Helpful Insights For Studying The Land of The Bible
Jewish Insights:

ONLINE RESOURCES FROM JEFF BAXTER

VIDEO WORKSHOPS & TRAINING
HELP! UNDERSTANDING REACHING TEENS & COLLEGE-AGED STUDENTS

SESSION 1

SESSION 2

VIDEO EPISODES ON REACHING THE NEXT GEN

NEXT GEN PODCAST
WITH JEFF BAXTER
W/ MISSION HILLS CHURCH PODCASTS

PARENTING

ABOUT JEFF BAXTER

Jeff Baxter is the Next Gen Pastor at Mission Hills Church in Littleton, CO (missionhills.org). He has been involved with Next Gen ministry for 25 years. He is a creative and passionate Bible teacher and life-long learner with advanced theological degrees (M.Div. D.Min). Jeff has served in all different churches in all different roles including Lead Pastor. He has traveled extensively oversees and taught at universities and conferences on theology, leadership and Next Gen ministry. He is married to beautiful Laurie and they have three awesome kids in high school and beyond. Look for Jeff at coffee shops for conversation and study or exploring the lands where the Bible look place like Israel, Greece, Turkey and Italy.

Web: JeffBaxter.org

To invite Jeff to speak at a church, retreat, conference, event or consult to help your church gain health and strategy particulary with the Next Generation or lead a tour to Israel for your group or church, please email him at.

Email: drjeffmbaxter@gmail.com

He would love to connect with you, especially over coffee!

BOOKS BY JEFF BAXTER

Found on Amazon

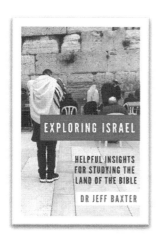

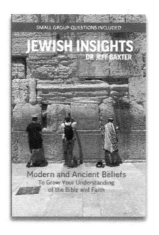

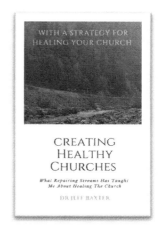

PARENTING

PARENTING

Made in the USA
Columbia, SC
17 February 2024